UNDERSTANDING the ATONEMENT
The Heart of Classic Methodist Theology

Vic Reasoner

2120 Culverson Ave
Evansville, IN 47714-4811

© 2025 Victor Paul Reasoner
ISBN 979-8-9937696-1-5
Library of Congress Control Number:
2025950017

Table of Contents

Understanding the Atonement 4
The Concept of Atonement in the Old Testament . 8
The Doctrine of Atonement in the New Testament 13
A Theology of Atonement 18
- The Atonement is Universal 19
- The Atonement is Substitutionary 27
- The Atonement is Satisfaction 34
  - The Concept of Propitiation 38
  - The Value of the Blood 41
- The Atonement is the Ultimate Exhibition of Divine Love 44
- Satan Was Defeated at the Cross 48

Unconditional Benefits of the Atonement 54
Conditional Benefits of the Atonement 57
Is Physical Healing Provided in the Atonement? . 57
Future Benefits of the Atonement 63
Bibliography 67

Understanding the Atonement

The atonement is the heart of the gospel. According to Eldon Dunlap, the entire theological enterprise of early Methodism

> was motivated by an evangelical zeal. The salvation of souls was their passion, and salvation rooted firmly in the reality and efficacy of the Atonement. The Atonement was the heart of their theology; it was the theme of their preaching; and it was the practical ground of their Christian living and hope of glory.[1]

John Wesley wrote, "Indeed, nothing in the Christian system is of greater consequence than the doctrine of Atonement."[2]

The basis of our salvation is the grace of God through the atonement of Jesus Christ. Paul declared, "May I never boast except in the cross of our Lord Jesus Christ" (Gal 6:14). "Christ died for us" (Rom 5:8) is the most basic statement of the atone-

---

[1] Dunlap, "Methodist Theology in Great Britain," 100.

[2] Wesley, *Letter* to Mary Bishop, 7 Feb 1778.

ment. Yet the preaching of the cross is a stumbling block to the Jews and foolishness to the Greeks (1 Cor 1:23).

But we could never save ourselves. We are under the sentence of death. Our sin is rebellion against God. As sinners, we are under the wrath of God. "The sinful mind is hostile to God. It does not submit to God's law, nor can it do so" (Rom 8:7). There are over 580 references to the wrath of God in the Old Testament. Over twenty Hebrew words are used to express this wrath. "God is angry with the wicked every day" (Ps 7:11). We must flee the wrath to come (Matt 3:7). We need propitiation. While *propitiate* can carry a pagan meaning of appeasement, this meaning is foreign to the New Testament. Rather, it means that God satisfies the just demands of his holy law through Christ

However, the doctrine of total depravity teaches that we can do nothing to save ourselves. If we are saved, God must provide atonement. We can assume that he would not have paid the supreme price of his Son if a lesser price would have paid for our sins.

But if God is sovereign, why could he not forgive our sin without any atonement? Since all have sinned, surely God will "grade on the curve." He cannot. God is bound by his truthfulness and justice. Justice and holiness demand punishment. The demands of the law must be satisfied. Sin deserves punishment. God said the penalty for sin was death (Gen 2:17; Rom 6:23). He must keep his word, for he cannot lie (John 17:17; Rom 3:4; Titus 1:2; Heb 6:18). Thus, clemency would imply that God's word could not be trusted.

God was under no obligation to rescue us, but because of his love he chose to do so. However, his plan to save us must not violate his character or his word. "But the Lord Almighty will be exalted by his justice, and the holy God will show himself holy by his righteousness" (Isa 5:16).

The atonement was not a divine necessity since God was not obligated to redeem fallen humanity. But if we were ever to be saved, it *was* necessary. Richard Watson explained,

> If inferior means had been sufficient, then more was done by the Father, when he delivered up his Son for us, than was necessary, a conclusion of an impious character; and if the greatest possible gift was bestowed, then nothing less could have been effectual, and this was *necessary* to human salvation.[3]

Too often mercy and grace are pitted against justice. The result is a defective view of God. How can he be both just and the one who justifies guilty sinners (Rom 3:26)? He cannot gratify his love without satisfying his justice. Richard Treffry explained that the atonement of Christ was the grandest judicial proceeding that ever took place in the universe and the most convincing demonstration of the righteousness of God.

> Now, the great object of the atonement of Christ was to demonstrate the righteousness

---

[3]Watson, *Theological Institutes*, 2:104.

of God, and thus enable him, without any dishonor to his attributes and government, to show mercy to the sinner. I have before remarked, that the pardon of sin, as an act of prerogative, would practically annul the divine government. In order, therefore, that God might prove himself just as well as good, Christ was appointed to undergo, in his own person, the punishment due to our sin.[4]

In the atonement Christ offered, "Love and faithfulness meet together; righteousness and peace kiss each other" (Ps 85:10). God began laying the foundation for this atonement under the old covenant.

---

[4]Treffry, *Letters on the Atonement*, 117, 58.

The Concept of Atonement in the Old Testament

God began teaching the necessity of atonement as early as Genesis 3. While Adam and Eve were conscious of their guilt, they did not repent. Instead they attempted to cover themselves with fig leaves (v 7). God covered them with animal skins. Something living had to die to adequately cover the guilty pair. This was the first time Adam and Eve had ever encountered death. The sacrificial system delineated in the Old Testament was not invented by the Jews nor copied from the pagans. It was based on a direct revelation of God.

The Hebrew word כפר (*kaphar*) means *to cover*. It is first used in Genesis 6:14 to cover over the ark with pitch or tar. It was that covering that shielded Noah's family from the water of God's judgment, coming between death outside the ark and the salvation of Noah's family inside the ark.

Exodus 12 described the deliverance of Passover. A lamb without blemish is slain and its blood brushed on the door frames in the outline of the cross. According to 1 Corinthians 5:7 Jesus is our Passover lamb.

The priesthood was instituted in Exodus. Jesus Christ is both our great high priest and the sacrificial lamb. On the Day of Atonement (Lev 16), the high priest slew one goat and sprinkled its blood in the Holy of Holies. He laid his hands on the head of the other animal, the scapegoat, and confessed the sins of the people. This goat was led into the wilderness. This ritual symbolized imputation and substitution; the removal of guilt and the offering for sin.

Atonement was the basic principle underlying all blood sacrifices. Gleason Archer explained,

> In token of this substitution the offerer laid his hand upon the victim's head, thus identifying himself with it as his representative. To signify his acceptance of the just penalty of death, he himself slew his victim, and then turned it over to the priest for the completion of the ceremony.[5]

Yom Kippur (a variation of *kaphar*) is the Day of Atonement. In Leviticus 16 the verb *kaphar* occurs sixteen times. The purpose for the Day of Atonement was to provide a covering which protected Israel from the wrath of God. Sinful humanity does not need a covering of leaves or pitch. We need a blood covering.

The priestly ritual included sprinkling blood on the *mercy seat*. More literally, כפרת (*kapporeth*), the noun form, should be translated *the place of propitiation*. This noun occurs seven times in the same chapter. The mercy seat is referenced in Hebrews 9:5 where the Greek adjective ἱλαστήριον (*hilasterion*) is used to refer to the lid on the ark of the covenant.

---

[5]Archer, *Survey of Old Testament Introduction*, 231.

This word also refers to propitiation. According to Leviticus 16:2, God appeared in a cloud of glory situated over this mercy seat. We cannot experience his Shekinah presence without the covering of his atonement.

Leviticus 17:11 explains that the life of a creature is in the blood. God said, "I have given it to you to make atonement for yourselves." Treffry wrote, "Nothing, surely, can more clearly convey the notion of transfer and substitution."[6]

The blood explains why Abel's sacrifice was accepted (Heb 11:4). The Greek word for *sacrifice*, θυσία (*thusia*), is based on the verb which means to slay or kill. It implies a violent act. *Blood* is a metaphor for death. Yet the blood of bulls and goats can never adequately substitute for human sin (Heb 10:4).

In Numbers 21 the people of Israel were dying from snake bites. The Lord told Moses to make a bronze snake and put it up on a pole. Anyone who was bitten could look at it and live. This deliverance symbolized Jesus hanging on the cross. Jesus taught, "Just as Moses lifted up the snake in the desert, so the Son of Man must be lifted up" (John 3:14). "But I, when I am lifted up from the earth, will draw all men to myself. He said this to show the kind of death he was going to die" (John 12:32-33).

Through this symbol God taught that sin is like a fatal snakebite. The snake on the cross represents the antidote. To this day the caduceus is used as the symbol for medical help. Christ took our punishment into his own body in order to produce a cure for sin.

---

[6]Treffry, *Letters on the Atonement*, 96.

Jesus is the only physician who can cure his patients by taking their disease. "Christ redeemed us from the curse of the law by becoming a curse for us, for it is written: Cursed is everyone who is hung on a tree" (Gal 3:13). We must look to the cross to be saved. God sent his own Son in the likeness of sinful man to be a sin offering (Rom 8:3).

To use the figurative language of Genesis 3:15, the snake bit the heel of Jesus Christ. He took our punishment into his own body in order to produce a cure for sin. Medical laboratories search for someone who has contracted a specific disease, and from the blood of that person who has overcome they produce a serum for the victim. The blood of Jesus is the only antitoxin in the world that will cure the snakebite of sin.

The book of Ruth tells the story of a kinsman-redeemer. The Hebrew term גאל (*gaal*) describes a near relative who was responsible to buy back property which the family once owned. Thus, Boaz illustrates the fact that before Jesus Christ could become our redeemer he had to become our kinsman.

Prior to the atonement of Christ, sin, which was confessed to the priest and dealt with according to Levitical ritual, was not punished due to the forbearance of God. But their redemption was contingent upon the atonement of Christ (Heb 9:15) since it was impossible for the blood of bulls and goats to take away sins (Heb 10:4). According to Acts 17:30, God overlooked ignorance in times past, but now he commands all people everywhere to repent.

Romans 2:4 and 3:26 both use ἀνοχή (*anoche*) which means "a holding back." This was not so much forgiveness as the withholding of penalty.

Jews who lived by God's law and who relied on the sacrificial system to turn away God's wrath when they fell short, were accepted by God on the basis of the future atoning work of Christ. Neither did God impute sin to the pagans who were ignorant of his law (Rom 5:13; Acts 17:30), but followed the law as revealed to their conscience. They were also accepted by God on the basis of the atoning work of Christ. Yet God had something better (Heb 11:39-40).

The Doctrine of Atonement in the New Testament

The sacrifice of Christ was once for all (Heb 10:10). As both the High Priest and the sacrificial offering, he obtained eternal redemption (Heb 9:11-12).

In the New Testament the word *atonement* is found only once in the King James Version, at Romans 5:11. However, four Greek words are used in the New Testament, borrowed from the home, the temple, the court, and the marketplace, to illustrate the basic meaning of atonement. These metaphors do overlap, but the basis concepts remain:

- **Relational**. καταλλάσσω (*katallasso*) means to reconcile or make peace. It conveys the theme of restored relationship. Christ is the mediator (1 Tim 2:5). The result is fellowship. According to 2 Corinthians 5:19, God reconciled the world to himself in Christ. Thus, God is both the reconciler and the reconciled. This concept is conveyed in at-one-ment.

- **Sacrificial**. ἱλάσκομαι (*hilaskomai*) means to propitiate; to turn away the anger of God. Various forms of this word occur six times in the New

Testament. Christ was our merciful and faithful high priest who offered himself as the once and for all sacrifice for our sins, turning away the wrath of God. The result is forgiveness.

- **Legal.** παρακαλέω (*parakaleo*) means to make an appeal or act as an advocate. In the Old Testament the high priest not only offered the sacrifice, but he made intercession. According to 1 John 2:1, Jesus Christ speaks to the Father, our judge, in our defense. Christ Jesus who died is at the right hand of God (Rom 8:34; Heb 7:25, 9:24, 10:12). The result is satisfaction of divine law and our forensic justification.

- **Commercial.** λυτρόω (*lutroo*) means to redeem or ransom. It conveys the commercial theme. We are bought with a price (1 Cor 6:20). Christ gave himself for us to redeem us from all wickedness (Titus 2:14). Thus, he taught us to pray, "Forgive us our debts" (Matt 6:12). The verb ἀφίημι (*aphiemi*) is used in the New Testament both of the release from sin and the dismissal of a debt. The result is deliverance and freedom.

When Jesus declared, "It is finished" (John 19:30), he said τετέλεσται (*tetelestai*). This Greek word often appeared on receipts and could be interpreted as "paid in full."[7] Thus, the atonement can be understood as a satisfaction of the penalty for our sin debt,

---

[7]Moulton and Milligan, *Vocabulary of the Greek Testament*, 630.

so long as this metaphor is not distorted beyond its intended purpose.

"You were bought at a price" (1 Cor 7:23). Wrapped up in the word *redemption* is the idea of the payment of a price or a ransom. While ransom is still connected with satisfaction, this metaphor can be distorted. *Redemption* should not be interpreted to mean that we were ransomed from Satan, however. The Bible never speaks of a ransom paid to the devil. "The satisfaction is, therefore, to be made, . . . not to him who detains the captive, . . . but to him whose law has been violated."[8] God never owed the devil anything and doesn't do business with him. We were trapped by our sinful nature and Christ paid the price of our freedom. Thus, the satisfaction view corrects this distortion by clarifying that God paid the ransom to himself in order to satisfy his own justice. Stott explained,

> The cross was not a commercial bargain with the devil, let alone one which tricked and trapped him; nor an exact equivalent, a *quid pro quo* to satisfy a code of honor or technical point of law.[9]

Since Christ is God, his life was of infinite value. The payment of Christ was sufficient, but not an exact equivalent. The emphasis should not be upon the quantity of suffering, but the quality of the one

---

[8]Watson, *Theological Institutes*, 2:126.

[9]Stott, *The Cross of Christ*, 159.

suffering. The proper emphasis is not the extent of his suffering but the value of the sacrifice.

Benjamin Field wrote that the Scriptures never represent the death of Christ as a mere commercial transaction — the payment of so much money by one person for so much debt owed by another. Our relationship to God is that of sinners to an offended Judge, not debtors to a creditor. Field acknowledged that there is a similarity between a debtor and a sinner. While both the debtor and the sinner are acquitted, beyond this point the analogy vanishes.

> The atoning act of Christ consisted not, therefore, in paying a civil debt, giving precisely what the original obligation required, but in suffering "the just for the unjust." It was a *satisfaction*, the rendering of something in the place of what is due, with which the Lawgiver is content.[10]

Thomas Ralston also explained that the atonement satisfied the justice of God, but it was not the exact payment of our penalty. If God could prescribe the terms on which the substitute should be accepted, he can also stipulate the condition upon which pardon and salvation are to be extended. Therefore, God is not under any obligation to extend pardon and salvation absolutely and unconditionally to anyone.[11]

---

[10]Field, *The Student's Handbook*, 161-162. See also Steele, *Antinomianism Revived*, 60.

[11]Ralston, *Elements of Divinity*, 233-237.

Thomas Summers noted that if sin is a debt and Christ paid only for the sins of the elect, "then not one of them can be lost and not one of the reprobate can be saved." Or if the atonement, thus understood, was made for all men, as universalists hold, "all men must be saved — none can be lost." Neither repentance, faith, nor obedience could be required, for that would be a kind of double jeopardy. But Christ did not perform the duties God requires of us. It is our faith, not the holiness of Christ, which is imputed to us for righteousness.[12] Faith is not the exact equivalent of righteousness, but God accepts it as sufficient for him to impute righteousness to us.

---

[12]Summers, *Systematic Theology*, 1:249, 242.

A Theology of Atonement

The apostolic fathers tended to repeat the Scriptures related to the atonement without formulating a theological statement. However, all of the essential elements of a theology of the atonement were expressed or implied in their writings. Polycarp, Ignatius, Barnabas, and Clement of Rome clearly stated a vicarious satisfaction understanding.[13]

A proper view of the atonement takes into account the love of God and the wrath of God, the satisfaction of his law and moral government, substitution, the active/passive work of Christ, victory over Satan, and reconciliation with God.

It is crucial to understand that the atonement was objective, or directed toward God, in contrast to subjective concepts of the atonement which are directed toward mankind. Thus, an objective view sees the atonement as necessary for our salvation, while a subjective view sees the atonement as arbitrary.

Our understanding of the atonement needs to include five major concepts.

---

[13]Pope, *Compendium*, 2:299.

The Atonement is Universal

Jesus is the Lamb of God who takes away the sin of the world (John 1:29). "For God so loved the world that he gave his only begotten Son" (John 3:16). William Burt Pope declared, "We should take it for granted that so glorious a Person would not be sent on a partial and limited errand; that, supposing Him to visit this earth, He would embrace its whole compass in His mission."[14]

The burden of proof is for Calvinists to demonstrate why they can legitimately say that *world* means only the world of the elect. They typically point out that Christ laid down his life for his sheep (John 10:11) and that he died for his church (Eph 5:25), but they fail to demonstrate that atonement was made *only* for those who constitute his church. Their logic raises the suspicion that they believe the elect are actually saved by divine predestination.

According to 1 John 2:2, Christ is the propitiation for the sins of the *whole* world. John uses this word *world* (κόσμος - *kosmos*) twenty-three times in his first letter. The uniform meaning of the word is the entire unbelieving world, in contrast to the church or Christians. In the nearest context, the *whole world* is referenced in 1 John 5:19 and it does not describe the elect. The adjective ὅλος (*holos*) means all, the total, the entire, or the complete. "There is not one place in the entire NT where 'world' means 'church' or 'the

---

[14]Pope, *Compendium*, 2:295.

elect.'"[15] Grant Osborne concluded, "In John's writings *kosmos* occurs 115 times, always of the world of unbelievers who are hostile to God and yet are the object of God's love and mission."[16]

In Romans 5:17-21 *the many* describes the actual effect of Adam's disobedience and *the many* also describes the potential effect of Christ's obedience. Mickelsen argued that Paul has not changed the extent of *the many* on either side of this comparison.[17] In other words, Christ died for just as many as were polluted by the sin of Adam.

According to 2 Corinthians 5:14-19, Christ died for all in order to reconcile the world to God. Christ gave himself a ransom for all (1 Tim 2:6). There is no grammatical or contextual indication that πᾶς (*pas*) does not mean *everyone*. He tasted death for everyone (Heb 2:9).

Titus 2:11 teaches that preliminary grace has appeared to all for the purpose of bringing salvation. According to 2 Peter 3:9, God wants everyone to come to repentance. No valid distinction can be made between God's desires and his decrees. He does not have two wills. However, Thomas Schreiner attempted to make this argument.[18] John Piper also

---

[15]Elwell, "Extent of Atonement," 100.

[16]Osborne, *Perspectives on the Extent of the Atonement*, 108.

[17]Mickelsen, *Wycliffe Bible Commentary*, 1199.

[18]Schreiner, *1, 2 Peter, Jude*, 381-382.

does in his chapter, "Are There Two Wills in God."[19] Carl Trueman, while defending Calvinism, conceded that "there are no real practical gains to be made from the two-will idea."[20] However, Thomas Coke wrote, "He has no secret will contrary to, and inconsistent with his revealed will."[21]

Calvinists and Arminians debate whether the mission of Christ was to atone for the sins of the whole world or only for the elect. Arminians contend that the provision is for all, but it is effectual only for those who believe. Calvinism holds to a limited atonement, but often they prefer the terms *definite atonement* or *particular redemption*. At this point they conflate atonement with salvation.

Calvinism can produce a list of proof texts which they claim infer a limited atonement. Arminians can also produce their list of proof texts which they claim infer a universal atonement. However,

> The task of harmonizing those various Scriptures poses a far greater problem for those who hold to a limited atonement than it does to those who hold to an unlimited position. Those who hold to an unlimited atonement recognize that some Scriptures emphasize the fact that Christ died for the elect, for the church, and for individual believers. However, they point out that when those verses

---

[19] Schreiner and Ware, *Still Sovereign*, 122-124.

[20] Trueman, "Definite Atonement View," 30, 209-210.

[21] Coke, *Commentary*, 6:844.

single out a specific group they do not do so to the exclusion of any who are outside that group since dozens of other passages include them. The "limited" passages are just emphasizing one aspect of a larger truth. In contrast, those who hold to a limited atonement have a far more difficult time explaining away the "unlimited" passages.[22]

Calvinism, however, argues that Christ did not intend to die for everyone, but those he died for are actually and certainly saved. They make the benefit of salvation unconditional and definite for the elect, based on their interpretation of Romans 8:29-32 as a *golden chain* which cannot be broken.[23]

But we must distinguish between atonement *accomplished* and atonement *applied*. The atoning sacrifice was made for all and sufficient for all, but effective only for the faithful. It is accomplished for all, but applied and efficacious only for believers, that is, the elect.

Theologians like William Shedd, himself a Calvinist, agree. He wrote:

> Atonement in and by itself, separate from faith, saves no soul . . . It is only when the death of Christ has been actually confided in as atonement, that it is completely "set forth" as God's propitiation for sin. . . . It is not the

---

[22]Lightner, "For Whom Did Christ Die?" 166.

[23]Reasoner, "Golden Chain or Iron Padlock?" 1-2.

making of this atonement, but the *trusting* in it, that saves the sinner.[24]

Norman Douty, also a Calvinist, explained,

> Without these acts [repentance and belief], even the elect are only potentially the recipients of these benefits. [Until then] all of Christ's saving work is theirs only potentially. . . . His death has only provided these benefits for them; the application of them is contingent on their repentance and faith.[25]

Calvinist scholar Douglas Moo commented on Romans 3:24,

> The "price" connoted by the word "redemption" was "paid" at the cross in the blood of Christ, the redeeming work that the payment made possible is, like justification, applied to each person when he or she believes.[26]

Ben Witherington said,

> Paul believes that Christ died for the sins of all, not just for some subset of humanity called the elect. Christ's death is a sufficient

---

[24]Shedd, *Dogmatic Theology*, 2:440.

[25]Douty, *Did Christ Die Only for the Elect*, 43.

[26]Moo, *NICNT*, 230.

atonement for the sins of all human beings, but it is effective only for those who appropriate its benefits through faith, as [Rom 3:22] makes evident. God's saving righteousness, which is also his mercy through the death of Christ, does not automatically benefit a person. A person must believe to receive this benefit.[27]

John 3:18 declares that whoever believes in him is not condemned, but whoever does not believe stands condemned. Thus, faith is mandatary. Lightner continued,

> The cross does not apply its own benefits . . . No elect person was saved at the time of Christ's dying. All men, including the elect, live some part of their lives in open rebellion to God, thus demonstrating that the finished accomplishments of Calvary must be applied by faith to reach an individual before any saving value comes to that individual.[28]

Calvinism has the dilemma of trying to explain how to preach a bona fide offer of salvation to the whole world if only the elect can be saved. Here Berkhof resorted to the "secret council of God."[29] This echos Calvin's comment,

---

[27]Witherington, *Paul's Letter to the Romans*, 109-110.

[28]Lightner, *The Death Christ Died*, 97.

[29]Berkhof, *Systematic Theology*, 393-399.

> But it could be asked here, if God does not want any to perish, why is it that so many do perish? To this my answer is, that no mention is here made of the hidden purpose of God, according to which the reprobate are doomed to their own ruin, but only of his will as made known to us in the gospel. For God there stretches forth his hand without a difference to all, but lays hold only of those, to lead them to himself, whom he has chosen before the foundation of the world.[30]

If God has another side, so secret that it is not revealed in Scripture, how did Calvin know about it? When the logical inconsistencies of Calvinism threaten to destroy their whole system, they adopt a position of agnosticism. We are told God's election and human believing cannot be put into a logical relationship to one another.[31] When their golden chain of logic snaps, they dismiss logic and scold us for trying to grasp what is incomprehensible.

The majority position in the Christian church has been on the side of universal atonement.[32] Augustine was the only advocate of limited atonement in the early church, and he makes no explicit or extended defense of the position. Chris Bounds concluded that belief in unlimited atonement was the consensual

---

[30]Calvin, *Commentary*, 22:419-420.

[31]Carson, *Divine Sovereignty and Human Responsibility*, 201-222.

[32]Elwell, "Extent of Atonement," 100.

exegesis and understanding of the first five hundred years of Christianity.[33]

Wesley argued for the universal atonement because the prophets, Christ himself, and his apostles affirm it. There is not one Scripture that says he did not die for all or affirms that he died only for some. Any interpretation that *all men* means *all men of the elect* or that *the world* means only the world of believers is a "senseless evasion." God has commanded that the gospel should be preached to every creature. God calls all men everywhere to repent (Acts 17:30). Those who perish are damned for not believing in Christ; therefore he died for them or else they are damned for not believing a lie. Those who perish might have been saved (2 Thess 2:10).[34]

Adam Clarke argued that if humanity is of one race and if Christ took on himself the nature of man and in human nature made expiation for the sins of nature, then redemption is general and the benefits of his death must necessarily apply to every human being who has descended from Adam. All who share the human nature have a right to apply to God, by virtue of that redemption, for remission of sins.[35]

Fred Sanders concludes that objectively salvation is accomplished for all through the Son, but subjectively salvation is accomplished particularly when

---

[33]Bounds, "Scope of the Atonement in the Early Church Fathers," 26.

[34]McGonigle, *Sufficient Saving Grace*, 141-142.

[35]Clarke, "Fragment in Favor of General Redemption, *Works*, 8:439-440.

each person hears and responds to the gospel. This is what Pope meant by distinguishing between universal redemption in general and special redemption of the individual. It is also what Thomas Oden meant that the atonement is universal in it sufficiency and conditional in it efficacy. It is limited to those who accept God's offer of salvation through Christ.[36]

The Atonement Is Substitution

In 1098 Anselm, the Archbishop of Canterbury, wrote *Why the God-Man?* building on the groundwork laid by Athanasius seven hundred years earlier. James Denney called Anselm's book "the truest and greatest book on the atonement that has ever been written."[37]

Athanasius accepted the concept of substitutionary atonement and related the suffering of Christ to the satisfaction of divine law, not a ransom to Satan. He taught repentance alone was not sufficient for salvation because it does not satisfy divine justice.

This title, *Cur Deos Homo* (*Why the God-Man?*) indicates that Anselm's thesis is that the purpose of the incarnation was atonement. Thus, both the incarnation and the atonement were logical necessities. Anselm concluded,

If then, as we agree, it is necessary that that

---

[36]Sanders, "Wesleyan View," 169, 175.

[37]Denney, *The Death of Christ*, 188.

heavenly city be completed from among men, and this cannot occur unless the satisfaction we have spoken of before is made, and if no one but God can make that satisfaction and no one but man is obliged to make it, then it is necessary that a God-man make it.[38]

While *necessity* can be based simply on deductive logic, Thomas Noble explained that Anselm's necessity was based on revealed truth. Anselm was not providing a logical syllogism, but rather an internal coherence of the Christian faith in the cross of Christ.[39]

The Reformation theologians modified Anselm's doctrine to include the subjective element of faith. Anselm had never specified how the atonement is appropriated. Faith does not justify, but it accepts the substitute who does provide our justification.

We must avoid any concept of the atonement that results in automatic salvation. The atonement makes salvation possible for all but completed for none. The atonement makes us *savable*.

Calvinists object that there are no conditions to be met — salvation is wholly the work of God. They teach God's grace is irresistible. Eternal security is based upon the particular atonement for the elect. Jesus suffered the exact amount necessary to pay the sins of the elect. Since two people cannot be punished for the same offence, those for whom Christ died will

---

[38] Anselm, *Cur Deus Homo*, 2.6.

[39] Noble, "The 'Necessity' of Anselm," 66.

be saved.

But Richard Treffry, in his *Letters on the Atonement* (1839), explained the terms of the covenant:

- That there shall be no obligation on the sufferer.
- That he shall himself be the subject of reward.
- That the ends of justice shall be more fully answered by the suffering of the substitute than by that of the actual offender.
- That the offended party shall be satisfied with the substitute and shall afford sufficient evidence of his admission of it.
- That the offender shall accept the suffering of the substitute upon such terms as he shall be pleased to propose.[40]

Essentially, God has offered to accept the suffering of Christ in lieu of the eternal punishment of the human race. Christ offered himself as our substitute. In return, he becomes Lord over a redeemed race (Ps 110:1). However, each person must also accept the terms individually in order for God to declare him justified. There must be a voluntary agreement among all parties in this covenant of salvation. While a covenant is unconditional in the sense that it cannot be negotiated, it is conditional in the sense that it must either be ratified or rejected.

The payment of Christ is not reckoned to our account until we believe. This condition of faith is stated in Romans 3:25 and Galatians 3:14. According to 1 Timothy 4:10, Christ has provided universal

---

[40]Treffry, *Letters on the Atonement*, 118.

salvation, but it is realized only by those who believe.

There are only two ways the debt of sin could be paid. If punishment is inflicted upon the transgressor, the debt is satisfied and the sinner is destroyed. The only other way is through a substitute. If we are under the sentence of death and Christ gave his life so that we would not have to die, his substitutionary death makes it possible for us to live and be reconciled.

But not any substitute would be acceptable to God. Our substitute must be identified with the human race in order for there to be a transfer of sin's punishment. Hebrews 2:17 states that he had to be like us in every way in order to make atonement for us. He had to be our representative before he could become our substitute.

Our substitute could not himself be a sinner either or he, too, would stand in need of a substitute. One sinless human being would substitute for one sinful human being. However, there are no sinless humans. Any concept of salvation by human works is an insult to the value of Christ's sacrifice and his finished work. Therefore, according to Psalm 49:7, "No man can redeem the life of another or give to God a ransom for him." The following verse gives the reason, "The ransom for a life is costly, no payment is ever enough."

Only Christ qualifies as our substitute because he alone is fully human, yet sinless. The incarnation was necessary for this reason. "God made him who had no sin to be a sin offering for us, so that in him we might become the righteousness of God" (2 Cor 5:21). However, the incarnation limited Christ to becoming a substitute for the human race. No salvation was provided for fallen angels. In fact, even the holy angels long to stoop down and investigate the redemption provided for humanity (1 Pet 1:12).

Is it right for the innocent to suffer for the guilty? Jesus declared, "No one takes [my life] from me, but I lay it down of my own accord" (John 10:18). In this case the innocent volunteered and the judge accepted him as our substitute. They were both moved by love.

William Burt Pope wrote that the very heart of the doctrine of atonement is its substitutionary nature. If this is taken away, the whole vocabulary of the New Testament would have to be fundamentally changed.[41]

The concept of substitution is unique to the Bible. Oden pointed out that in the New Testament it is not humans who come to God with a compensatory gift, but rather God who comes to humanity in self-giving.[42] Treffry wrote,

> The doctrine of the atonement, if it be true, is to be found in the Bible, and in the Bible only. If God had not revealed it, we should never have conjectured anything resembling it. It is quite beyond the scope and range of human reason.[43]

Substitution is prefigured as early as Genesis

---

[41]Pope, *Person of Christ*, 50.

[42]Oden, *The Word of Life*, 352.

[43]Treffry, *Letters on the Atonement*, 13.

22:8. Substitution is clear foreseen by Isaiah 53:5. Alec Motyer wrote that "this verse cannot be understood without the idea of substitution."[44] According to Oden, there are eleven different metaphors for substitution in Isaiah 53.[45]

Matthew 20:28 and Mark 10:45 both teach that Christ came "to give his life as ransom *for* (ἀντί - *anti* - in place of) many." Romans 5:6-8 declares, "When we were still powerless, Christ died for (ὑπέρ - *huper* - in behalf of; for the sake of) the ungodly. . . . But God demonstrates his own love for [to] us in this: While we were still sinners, Christ died for (*huper*) us." In 1 Timothy 2:6 the text is clear that Christ paid the ransom himself in the place and on the behalf of (*huper*) all men. According to 1 Peter 2:24, he bore our sins in his body. Wesley explained, "that is the punishment due them."[46] In 1 Peter 3:18, Peter teaches that Christ suffered and died for sins once for all, the righteous for (*huper*) the unrighteous, not a repeated sacrifice every time the Mass is offered.

According to 2 Corinthians 5:21 Christ became a sin offering for (*huper*) us. This verse connects with Isaiah 53:10 where the Messiah is made a guilt or trespass offering. Leviticus 5:1-6:7 discusses the guilt offering. Motyer said it could be called the satisfaction offering.[47]

---

[44] Motyer, *TOTC*, 335.

[45] Oden, *The Word of Life*, 379.

[46] Wesley, *Notes*, 613.

[47] Motyer, *TOTC*, 18:338.

Watson was emphatic that Jesus did *not* become a sinner.[48] Wesley emphasized, "But it is never said, he 'was made a sinner.' Therefore, the expressions are not parallel. But he need not have been 'made sin' at all, if we had not been 'made sinners' by Adam."[49] Oden explained that while substitution did not make Christ a sinner, he was viewed and dealt with as such. He was not a sinner in our stead in the sense that he himself sinned.[50]

Commenting on Isaiah 53:4-5, Wesley wrote, "Our sins were the procuring cause of all his sufferings. His sufferings were the penal effects of our sins." Wesley continued,

> Every *chastisement* is for some *fault*. That laid on Christ was not for his own but ours, and was needful to reconcile an offended Lawgiver and offending guilty creatures to each other.[51]

Penal substitution means that Christ took upon himself our penalty for sin. Penal satisfaction means that as our substitute he satisfied the just demands of the law. However, the two terms, satisfaction and substitution, are often confused. Properly understood, they illustrate the role of Christ as the mediator be-

---

[48] Watson, *Theological Institutes*, 2:163-164.

[49] Wesley, *BE Works*, 12:225-226.

[50] Oden, *The Word of Life*, 384.

[51] Wesley, *BE Works*, 12:420-421.

tween God and man.

The Atonement Is Satisfaction

Penal satisfaction is *objective*. Its object is to satisfy the justice of God. The purpose of Christ's substitution was to provide satisfaction. "He shall see the travail of his soul and be satisfied. By his knowledge my righteous Servant shall justify many"(Isa 53:11). The death of Christ is both a demonstration of God's love and the satisfaction of God's law.

John Stott observed that "no two words in the theological vocabulary of the cross arouse more criticism than 'satisfaction' and 'substitution.'"[52]

Summers wrote that the propitiatory sacrifice of Christ embraced the "twofold idea of satisfaction and substitution." Summers went on to say that 1 Peter 2:22-24, 3:18 taught satisfaction; Christ suffered for (περί - *peri*) sins; it taught substitution, the just for (ὑπέρ - *huper*); and it taught reconciliation, in order that (ἵνα - *hina*) he might bring us to God.[53] H. Orton Wiley also conceded that the two words substitution and satisfaction necessarily belong to the word atonement.[54]

Anselm viewed sin as a debt, based on the word in the Lord's prayer. God cannot just arbitrarily forgive. The debt remains unpaid. Punishment could be

---

[52]Stott, *The Cross of Christ*, 111.

[53]Summers, *Systematic Theology*, 1:225-228.

[54]Wiley, *Christian Theology*, 2:282.

inflicted upon the transgressor, but then no one could be saved. The only other way the debt can be paid is through a substitute. According to Psalm 49:7 the payment offered must be greater than the total of all finite creation. Only deity can satisfy this claim, but only humanity can render the satisfaction for his own sin. Thus, the satisfaction must be rendered by the God-man whose satisfaction is greater than our sin and is accepted by God.

Anselm's concept of satisfaction was expanded by Bonaventure, who taught that it was fitting for humanity to be restored by God. If God does not restore us, it cannot be done. There is no more fitting method for restoring humanity than by a satisfaction of justice. This maintains the balance between God's attributes of justice, wisdom, omnipotence, and majesty. He is both merciful and just.

However, it was necessary that God be just, not just that he show mercy. Yet, a sinless creature could not render satisfaction for the whole human race. A single creature is finite and on a level with all other finite creatures. Infinity alone can save us. Sinful man cannot make satisfaction for his own sin, because he would then incur eternal death and could not be redeemed. God was obligated to accept the satisfaction made by Christ, however, since he was behind the offer. Thus, the satisfaction of Jesus Christ is the most fitting and only way atonement could be made.

Benjamin Field wrote,

> If God is to extend forgiveness to the guilty, it must be in a way that will satisfy the

claims of infinite justice, and thus maintain in their full dignity, free from every charge of imperfection and mutability, the character of the Governor, the rectitude of His administration, and the sanction of His law.[55]

Wesley's concept of the atonement is essentially Anselm's view. Some Wesleyan theologians have objected to the penal satisfaction theory of the atonement on the basis that it leads either to universalism or a limited atonement. In other words, if Christ paid the penalty for the sins of the world then the whole world will finally be saved. The other option is that Christ only paid the penalty for the sins of the elect. However, William Abraham stated that Wesley accepted a version of penal substitution, "refusing to accept the ensuing logic that readily led to either limited atonement or universalism."[56]

John Wesley did not hold to either universalism or a limited atonement. He explained that Christ made a full satisfaction for the sins of the world, that th wrath of God was appeased, and justice is satisfied.[57]

The central point of the Penal Substitutionary Theory was of great importance for Wesley. Christ is the satisfier of our sin and guilt, the One who died as the sacrifice to

---

[55]Field, *The Student's Handbook*, 205.

[56]Abraham, "Atonement," 72.

[57]Wesley, *Notes*, 244, 631, 371.

satisfy the divine wrath and to provide for our forgiveness by the infinite value of his sacrifice in satisfaction of God's justice.[58]

Wesley differed from Calvinism at two points: the work of Christ is universal in its extent; and the work of Christ is conditional, becoming effectual only if it is accepted by faith. The atonement was not unconditional salvation nor was it an alternative to the penalty. Rather, it was a conditional offer of redemption to all who accept Jesus Christ as their substitute.

Wesley described the atonement as "satisfaction for the sins of the whole world."[59] James Arminius taught that God

> rendered satisfaction to *his Love for Justice and to his Hatred against sin,* when he imposed on his Son the office of Mediator by the shedding of his blood and by the suffering of death; and he was unwilling to admit him as the Intercessor for sinners except when sprinkled with his own blood in which he might be made the propitiation for sins. . . . In this respect also it may with propriety be said, that God rendered satisfaction to himself, and appeased himself in "the Son of his

---

[58] Williams, *John Wesley's Theology Today*, 83. I think Williams should have said "penal *satisfaction.*"

[59] Wesley, "God's Love to Fallen Man," Sermon #59, 1.3; "End of Christ's Coming," Sermon #62, 2.6; "Spiritual Worship," Sermon #77, 1.7.

love."[60]

Amos Binney explained that God was just in punishing sin and as justifying the sinner because "Christ thus became the sinner's substitute, and his death a satisfaction to justice."[61]

The Concept of Propitiation

"And he himself is the propitiation for our sins, and not for ours only but also for the sins of the whole world" (1 John 2:2). The purpose of propitiation is satisfaction, and satisfaction was provided through substitution.

Propitiation is part of satisfaction. In his comments on Romans 3:25, Wesley wrote that Christ's propitiatory sacrifice was made to "appease an offended God. But if, as some teach, God never was offended, there was no need of this propitiation. And if so, Christ died in vain."[62] Here Wesley was pushing back against William Law. In a letter, Wesley explained,

> Had God never been angry, he could never have been reconciled. . . . Although therefore I do not term God (as Mr. Law supposes) "a wrathful being," which conveys the wrong idea; yet I firmly believe that he was angry

---

[60] Arminius, *Works*, 2:221-222.

[61] Binney, *TPC*, 403.

[62] Wesley, *Notes*, 370.

with all mankind, and that he was reconciled to them by the death of his Son. And I know that he *was* angry with *me* till I believed in the Son of his love. And yet this is no impeachment to his mercy, that he is just as well as merciful.[63]

Richard Watson explained,

To propitiate is to appease, to turn away the wrath of an offended person. In this case the wrath to be turned away is the wrath of God. Not that he is implacable, the unfounded objection which many bring against the doctrine of the atonement. There is not only no implacability in God, but a most tender affection toward the sinning race, which is proved by the gift of his Son. This is the most eminent proof of his love, that for our sakes "he spared not his own Son."[64]

More recently, Ben Witherington conceded, "It is hardly possible to remove the notion of anger or wrath and the notion of appeasement or satisfaction from these discussions, and have anything significant left to say about the atonement . . . Sins do not need atoning for, if God does not need to be propitiated."[65]

---

[63]Wesley, *Letter* to Mary Bishop, 7 Feb 1778.

[64]Watson, *Exposition*, 493.

[65]Witherington, "Death of Sin in the Death of Jesus," 8, 18.

In his notes on 1 John 2:2, Wesley explained that because Jesus is the propitiation, "the wrath of God is appeased."[66] Wesley noted on 2 Corinthians 5:21 that we "must have been consumed by the Divine justice, had not this atonement been made for our sins."[67] At 1 Peter 2:24 Wesley commented that Christ bore our sins, "that is, the punishment due them."[68]

The purpose of propitiation was the *satisfaction* of the justice of God. Numbers 35:30-33 taught that no ransom or satisfaction was acceptable for a murderer. Three times in this passage the Hebrew word for atonement, *kopher*, was used.

Properly understood, *propitiation* does not describe an act of appeasement to a pagan deity in an attempt to "get on his good side"; it refers to the satisfaction of divine justice. Stott pointed out that in a pagan context it is always humans who seek to avert divine anger either through rituals, magic, or sacrifices. However, the biblical doctrine of propitiation is based on the premise that we can do nothing to compensate for our sins or turn away God's anger. Therefore, God takes the initiative and himself provides the propitiation in the person of his Son.[69]

"The life of a creature is in the blood, and I have given it to you to make atonement for yourselves on

---

[66]Wesley, *Notes*, 631.

[67]Wesley, *Notes*, 458.

[68]Wesley, *Notes*, 613.

[69]Stott, *The Cross of Christ*, 173-175.

the altar; it is the blood that makes atonement for one's life" (Lev 17:11). "Without the shedding of blood there is no forgiveness" (Heb 9:22). However, "It is impossible for the blood of bulls and goats to take away sins" (Heb 10:4). Therefore, a body was prepared for Christ (v 5).

It was not his teaching, his moral example, his obedient life, or his sufferings that saved us. We are saved through his blood. Salvation comes from the atonement, not the incarnation. The Methodist Conference in 1871 declared, "We still 'preach Christ,' as against science and philosophy: we preach 'Christ *crucified*,' as against those who misplace and exaggerate the Incarnation."[70]

Richard S. Taylor explained,

> If Christ's blood was not primarily penal in nature and directly a means of satisfying the moral and legal claims against the sinner, but rather merely a means of proclaiming God's wrath against sin for the sake of upholding moral government, then the connection between Christ's death and the Old Testament breaks down.[71]

The Value of the Blood

Blood is a metonymy or synecdoche for *atonement*. In other words, to speak of *the blood* is to uti-

---

[70]Gregory, "Annual Address of the Conference to the Methodist Societies," 835. See also Tooley, "Reinventing Redemption," 131-132.

[71]Taylor, *God's Integrity and the Cross*, 96.

lize a figure of speech in reference to the atonement, in order to emphasize substitution by using a more forceful word.

First Peter 1:19 calls the blood of Christ *precious.* Blood represents life, and for Christ to shed his blood means that he had to die. To pay the price in blood was to pay with your life. Jesus had to die a violent death to redeem us with his blood.[72] His blood is our ransom price (Acts 20:28; 1 Cor 6:20; 1 Peter 1:18-20; Col 1:14, some mss v 20). Through the blood we are redeemed from the guilt and power of sin.

- The blood makes propitiation (Rom 3:25); it satisfied the justice of God (Isa 53:11). It is the blood applied that turns away the judgment of God. God promised, "When I see the blood I will pass over you" (Exod 12:13).
- We are justified by his blood (Rom 5:9).
- We have redemption through the blood (Eph 1:7). This states the cost of the atonement.
- We are brought near through the blood of Christ (Eph 2:13). It is the blood applied that marks us as owned by God; we have been purchased by God and Satan has no claim on us. Acts 20:28 refers to the church which Christ purchased with his own blood.
- The blood provides reconciliation (Col 1:20).
- The blood ratified and inaugurated the new covenant between God and his people (Heb 9:16-18).
- The blood gives us access to the presence of God (Heb 10:19).

---

[72]Morris, *The Atonement*, 52-65.

- The blood makes us holy (Heb 13:12).
- The blood purifies us from all sin (1 John 1:7). Zechariah prophesied, "On that day a fountain will be opened to the house of David and the inhabitants of Jerusalem, to cleanse them from sin and impurity" (13:1). Revelation 7:14 describes a multitude who have washed their robes and made them white in the blood of the Lamb.
- We are washed in the blood (Rev 1:5, some texts have *freed us*).
- The blood makes us overcomers (Rev 12:11).

First Peter 1:2 says that we are "sprinkled" by his blood. At Mt Sinai the people entered into covenant with God (Exod 24:3-8). Moses took the blood of bulls and sprinkled half of it on the altar. He read the covenant to the people and when they agreed to it, he sprinkled them with the other half of the blood. The book of Hebrews picks this up and teaches that the blood of Christ sprinkles the altar in heaven, the very throne of God. This satisfies God's justice and makes atonement for our sins. This is what happened at the Passover when blood was sprinkled on the door post to outline a cross and the death angel passed over.

But we are sprinkled with the other half to mark God's claim upon us. Through the sprinkling of this blood we enter into covenant with God. The blood of Jesus does more than pay the penalty for our sin; it actually makes us part of God's family. We are connected with Christ and are to abide in him as the vine and branches are connected.

In the Lord's Supper, just as the bread represents our participation in the body of Christ, so the cup represents our fellowship in the blood of Christ (1 Cor 10:16). Moses said, "This is the blood of the covenant that the Lord has made with you" (Exod 24:8). Jesus said, "This cup is the new covenant in my blood" (1 Cor 11:25). Unless you drink his blood, you have no life in you (John 6:53).

The Atonement Is the Ultimate Exhibition of Divine Love

In his sermon on John 3:16, Adam Clarke preached:

> It is here asserted that the *love of God* was the spring and source of human redemption and when we consider the fallen degraded and corrupt state of the human race we may rest satisfied that *there* it must originate or no where. Man could no claim on the holiness or justice of his Maker because he had swerved from His allegiance and broken His law nor can we conceive that any other attribute of the Divine Nature could be excited in his behalf.[73]

Although God foreknew who would believe, he provided a universal atonement which demonstrates the extravagance of his love. And he receives the maximum glory from the millions who freely chose to serve him, even though they had the power of contrary choice.

---

[73]Clarke, "The Love of God to a Lost World," *Works,* 3:66.

Calvinism, on the other hand, emphasizes limited atonement by saying that God gets exactly what he paid for. If he paid for the salvation of ten souls, then ten souls are saved. That view suggests the miserliness of his love.

While his anger is righteous, his justice is tempered by love. He should not be characterized as a bloodthirsty tyrant who would have destroyed the human race had Jesus not come between and bore the brunt of his rage. God is love, but he cannot be reduced to simply one attribute. His wrath is his resistance to everything unholy. Both his love and his wrath are holy. The problem is not with God; the problem is with humanity.

The atonement is the revelation of God's glory, his justice, his mercy, his wisdom, his power, and his love. Nor can God the Father be depicted as different from God the Son, since the Son is the perfect representation of the Father.

James Denney argued, "If the propitiatory death of Jesus is eliminated from the love of God, it might be unfair to say that the love of God is robbed of all meaning, but it is certainly robbed of all its apostolic meaning."[74]

Thus, atonement is a holy love which provides a substitute. However, some have emphasized the subjective influence of this love at the expense of the objective, legal efficacy of the substitutionary atonement.

We must emphasize that Christ died because of our sin against God *and* because of God's love toward

---

[74]Denney, *Atonement and the Modern Mind*, 58.

us. These contrasting emphases were represented by two medieval theologians of the twelfth century. While Anselm taught satisfaction, Abelard taught the efficacy of the atonement was largely the moral influence it exerts. Stott concluded, "In general terms, Anselm was right to understand the cross as a satisfaction for sin, but he should have laid more emphasis on God's love. Abelard was right to see the cross as a manifestation of love, but wrong to deny what Anselm affirmed. . . . For it was precisely in making a just satisfaction for sin that the manifestation of love took place."[75]

I realize that this demonstration of God's love is subjective — meaning it is directed toward mankind. Yet Scripture is emphatic, "Greater love has no one than this that someone lay down his life for his friends" (John 15:13). "But God shows his love for us in that while we were still sinners, Christ died for us" (Rom 5:8).

While the wrath of God has already been referenced as the basis for propitiation, it is helpful to realize that

> God's wrath is not the opposite of his love: it is the form which his holy love takes against anything which corrupts and destroys the creatures he has so lovingly created. To speak of the wrath of God is to speak of the blazing fire of that holy love which destroys

---

[75]Stott, *The Cross of Christ*, 221.

everything which is evil.[76]

The danger is in making this the *only* reason for atonement. When this is done, atonement is reduced to a moral influence. The moral influence model of atonement, advocated early on by Peter Abelard (1079-1142), says that Christ died on the cross in order to demonstrate God's love which should inspire moral transformation within humanity. However, it remains rather vague regarding how the violent death of Christ actually demonstrates God's love. Could not God have shown his love in other ways?

The theory also says that the death of Christ should inspire humanity to repent and live morally. In response, Anselm replied, "You have not yet considered the seriousness of sin."[77] In other words, we need more than an example to inspire us.

As Paul discovered, the harder he tried to do what was right, the more he realized he was bound by sin. He approved of righteousness, but was powerless to live righteous in his own strength (Rom 7:16). We all need more than the inspiration of a moral example — we need a Savior from sin. God so loved us in our helpless condition that he proved a substitute.

A more conservative form of moral influence is moral government, first championed by Hugo Grotius (1583-1645) and revived by John Miley (1879). In this view God had no intrinsic need to punish us before

---

[76]Noble, *Christian Theology*, 1.3.786.

[77]Anselm, *Cur Deus Homo?* 1.21.

forgiving us. However, he needed to emphasize the seriousness of sin by making an example through the sufferings of Jesus. Thus, there is tension between God as father and as governor. If punishment is not administered when a command is broken, we lose respect for the law and society would break down. God demonstrates how serious sin is through the greatness of the sacrifice he required.

While such an emphasis reinforces our fear of sin, it provides no basis for forgiveness or deliverance from sin. Thus, the punishment of Christ might make a profound impression on the sinner, but could not act as a deterrent if we are sinful by nature.

Satan was defeated at the cross

Christ triumphed over the claims of Satan (1 Cor 15:24-25; Col 2:15). According to Revelation 12:7-9 the first phase of the cosmic battle takes place in heaven between Michael, the guardian of God's people, and the dragon, who is Satan.

However, Revelation 12:10-12 describe a second defeat at the time salvation and the kingdom of God came. This second demotion corresponds to Luke 10:28, where Jesus, in anticipation, said, "I saw Satan fall like lightning from heaven." It also corresponds to John 12:31, "Now is the time for judgment on this world; now the prince of this world will be driven out."

This description cannot be the primordial battle when Satan initially fell, because such a view conflicts with the consequences of vv 10-12. Satan, who had already lost his position in heaven, was now cast out of heaven. Satan fell at the beginning of the first creation and falls again at the start of the new creation.

According to Revelation 12:10, "Now the accuser, who accused night and day is cast down." *Now* is ἄρτι (*arti*), a temporal adverb. Along with the aorist verb, *became*, John clearly records that salvation has been provided and the kingdom has been established at the time of his vision in the first century. We overcome by the atoning blood of the Lamb (v 11).

"And having disarmed the powers and authorities, he made a public spectacle of them, triumphing over them by the cross" (Col 2:15). Christ descended into the regions of death to proclaim his victory. He made a public spectacle of his booty, like Roman armies who marched their prisoners through the streets of Rome. The Greek verb θριαμβεύω (*thriambeuo*) was used to describe a Roman procession with its parade of captives. Wesley stated, "He triumphed over all his enemies, Satan, sin, and death, which had before enslaved all the world." Christ first conquered Satan, then sin in his death, and finally death in his resurrection.[78]

Daniel 7:21-27 describes the ascension and session of Christ. At the resurrection and ascension of Christ back to heaven the Father told him, "Sit at my right hand until I make your enemies a footstool for your feet" (Ps 110:1). The legal case has already been decided against Satan. Christ has regained control and we are seated with him (Eph 2:6). "In the mighty works of Jesus the power of the Kingdom has broken

---

[78]Wesley, *Notes*, 496, 442.

into the world; Satan has met his match; the cosmic end-struggle has begun."[79]

At the cross Satan received a mortal wound to his head. He is terminally ill, but not yet dead. He is alive, but not well, on planet earth.[80] His time is short (Rev 12:12). Demonic activity has been limited. Athanasius wrote *On the Incarnation of the Word of God* in the fourth century.

> Since the Savior has come among us, idolatry not only has no longer increased, but what there was is diminishing and gradually coming to an end: and not only does the wisdom of the Greeks no longer advance, but what there is is now fading away: And demons, so far from cheating any more by illusions and prophecies and magical arts, if they so much as dare to make the attempt, are put to shame by the sign of the Cross. And to sum the matter up: behold how the Savior's doctrine is everywhere increasing, while all idolatry and everything opposed to the faith of Christ is daily dwindling, and losing power, and falling. And thus beholding, worship the Savior "Who is above all" and mighty, even God the Word; and condemn those who are being worsted and done away by Him. For as,

---

[79] Bright, *The Kingdom of God*, 218.

[80] Contrary to Hal Lindsey, *Satan is Alive and Well on Planet Earth* (1972); see Grider, *Wesleyan-Holiness Theology*, 170.

when the sun is come, darkness no longer prevails, but if any be still left anywhere it is driven away; so, now that the divine Appearing of the Word of God is come, the darkness of the idols prevails no more, and all parts of the world in every direction are illuminated by His teaching.[81]

Satan's power has been broken. Summers wrote,

That evil angels and evil men are permitted to employ the agencies of nature for malevolent purposes is true; but this is only within a very limited and prescribed range, controlled and overruled for wise and benevolent ends, by the one only Creator, Proprietor, and Preserver of the universe.[82]

The victory of the cross is the *decisive* victory of Christ over Satan. The victory of the Christian church, through the atonement of Christ and enforced through our testimony, amounts to the *progressive* victory of Christ until his return. We live between those two great events. Satan has been in check mate since the cross.

Oscar Cullman developed the analogy of D-Day and V-Day to explain the decisive and the *final* vic-

---

[81] Athanasius, *Incarnation of the Word*, § 55; *NPNF*2 4:66. John of Damascus recorded a similar statement in the eighth century [*On the Orthodox Faith*, 4.4; *NPNF*2 9:75].

[82] Summers, *Systematic Theology*, 1:73.

tory of Christ. Based on World War 2 history, D-Day was the victory of the cross. However, the battle was not over at D-Day. Yet the second world war turned at D-Day from a defensive battle to an offensive battle — which culminated at V-Day.[83]

The third and final defeat of Satan is described in Revelation 20:10. In the meantime the church must resist and stand (Eph 6:11,13). We are able to withstand, and when the battle is over we can still be standing. The believer has authority over Satan and his kingdom, since we are seated with Christ (Eph 2:6).

The heathen still rage (Ps 2:1) and the devil still roars (1 Pet 5:8), and we do not yet see everything subject to Christ (Heb 2:8), but no weapon forged against us will prevail (Isa 54:17). If we resist the devil, he will flee (Jas 4:7). C. S. Lewis warned,

> There are two equal and opposite errors into which our race can fall about devils. One is to disbelieve in their existence. The other is to believe, and to feel an excessive and unhealthy interest in them. They themselves are equally pleased by both errors and hail a materialist or a magician with the same delight.[84]

At the second coming the devil will be thrown into the lake of fire and brimstone and be tormented day and night forever and ever (Rev 20:10). This is

---

[83] Ladd, *The Last Things*, 47.

[84] Lewis, *Screwtape Letters*, 3.

the final victory. Martin Luther wrote sometime between 1527-1529,

> And though this world, with devils filled,
> Should threaten to undo us,
> We will not fear, for God hath willed
> His truth to triumph through us.
> The Prince of Darkness grim,—
> We tremble not for him;
> His rage we can endure,
> For lo! His doom is sure,—
> One little word shall fell him.

That one little word is the name of Jesus. It is the name above all earthly powers, and his kingdom is forever.

I am aware that the Christus Victor model of atonement was put forward by Gustaf Aulén in 1931. This was a development of the writings of Irenaeus, an early church father. Martin Luther also emphasized the atonement as victory over Satan. The danger of adopting this approach exclusively is that it reduces the atonement to this one aspect. But it is valid to incorporate it as one aspect of atonement theology. When it is advocated at the expense of the other aspects of atonement, it tends to emphasize that we are victims who need to be rescued instead of sinners who need to be forgiven. Actually, both descriptions are true.

Unconditional Benefits of the Atonement

The optimism of Methodism is grounded in the conviction that universal grace restores human personality to native dignity, human responsibility to everlasting reality, and human perfection to gracious possibility.[85]

"Every blessing known to man is the result of the purchase price of our Lord Jesus Christ, and comes down from the Father of lights."[86] Unconditional benefits of Christ's atonement include a suspension of the death penalty. The human race was allowed to continue since the penalty for sin, physical death, would be satisfied in the death of Christ. The continued existence of the human race is a benefit of the atonement. However, Adam and Eve died spiritually when they sinned.

Unconditional benefits of Christ's atonement also include the salvation of all who die before reaching an age of responsibility. Original guilt is not imputed. Calvinism has traditionally held that only elect infants go to heaven when they die. Fletcher observed that in his day Calvinists were beginning to teach that all infants were elect, but when they grew up

---

[85]Scott, "Methodist Theology in America," 265.

[86]Wiley, *Christian Theology*, 2:297.

they were not necessarily so.[87] Historically, Calvinism has held that children of believers are elect. Other Calvinists hold that all babies are elect. However, since everyone came into this world as an infant, and since this decree of election and reprobation supposedly occurred either before creation or after the fall, how can the same individual be elect as an infant and potentially reprobate as an adult?

The restoration of all men to a state of salvability is an unconditional benefit. Although we are totally depraved, we are also under preliminary grace. Thus, preliminary grace is an unconditional benefit of the atonement.

> For allowing that all the souls of men are dead in sin by *nature*, this excuses none, seeing there is no man that is in a state of mere nature; there is no man, unless he has quenched the Spirit, that is wholly void of the grace of God. No man living is entirely destitute of what is vulgarly called "natural conscience." But this is not natural; it is more properly termed "preventing grace."[88]

Calvinism also teaches that *common grace* is an unconditional benefit of the atonement. Gary North explained, "God gives rebels enough rope to hang themselves for all eternity. This is the fundamental

---

[87] Fletcher, *Works*, 1:284-285.

[88] Wesley, "Working Out Our Own Salvation," Sermon #85, 3.4.

implication of the doctrine of common grace."[89] This is essentially a restraint upon the wicked.

Thus, for Calvinists the atonement provides collective benefits for all mankind, but the atonement is salvific only for the elect. Thus, common grace does not lead to salvation in Calvinistic theology. However, according to Romans 2:4 the purpose of God's kindness is to lead us toward repentance. We need not reject the doctrine of common grace, which includes the positive blessings stated in Matthew 5:45. But unlike the exclusive nature of Calvinistic theology, the purpose of all grace is to lead toward salvation. Thus, for Wesleyan theology preliminary grace is a more extensive term. Allan Coppedge explained,

> The difference between Wesley's prevenient grace and the Calvinists' common grace was that while both provided a restraining influence on the evil in human beings so that society could exist, prevenient grace also restored the capacity of every man to accept salvation, whereas common grace did not.[90]

According to Oden, common grace "enables society to live together in a proximately just and orderly manner, and enables it to cultivate scientific, rational, and economic pursuits of civilization."[91]

---

[89]North, "Common Grace, Eschatology, and Biblical Law," 17.

[90]Coppedge, *John Wesley in Theological Debate*, 136.

[91]Oden, *Transforming Power of Grace*, 63.

Conditional Benefits of the Atonement

The entire plan of salvation: reconciliation, redemption, justification, regeneration, sanctification, glorification — everything going forward in the order of salvation hinges on the atonement.

Is physical healing provided in the atonement?

Sin alone requires atonement. Must the wrath of God be turned away because we are sick? Do we need reconciliation because we are ill? Is redemption necessary in order to be healed? Is sickness the breach of divine law which must be satisfied through a substitute?

However, we know that sickness, disease, and even death came into this world as the result of sin. Christ came to destroy the hold of sin on our life. Ultimately we will be delivered from the effects of sin when we get an immortal body. The curse of sin is being broken. In this life we can be delivered from the power of sin, but not necessarily from all infirmities. We do not declare to God that he must heal us. Gordon Fee declared, "God *must* do *nothing*! God is free to be God. He is sovereign in all things and is simply not under our control. . . . Healing, therefore, is not a divine obligation; it is a divine gift."[92]

However, God does heal often because of his love and grace. The basis for praying for divine healing is God's nature, as well as the gifts of the Spirit, not

---

[92]Fee, *Disease of the Health and Wealth Gospel*, 31.

Christ's atonement or the intensity of our faith. According to Exodus 15:26 it is God's nature to heal.

The healing referred to in Isaiah 53:4-5 is spiritual healing. In Matthew 8:16-17 when Jesus cast out demons and healed the sick, Matthew said this was in fulfillment of Isaiah 53:4. Adam Clarke explained that while Isaiah was describing the taking away of sin through the atonement, these acts of healing and deliverance were symbolic of salvation.[93]

Millard Erickson concluded that Isaiah is referring to physical and mental illnesses. The Hebrew word for grief (חלי - *chali*) is predominately used for physical sickness and the word for sorrows (מכאוב - *makov*) conveys the idea of mental pain, sorrow, or distress. However, Isaiah does not say that Jesus has vicariously borne them in our place. Rather, he entered into the same conditions we experience through his incarnation and thus he is able to sympathize with us.[94]

An old Negro spiritual says "There is a Balm in Gilead." *Balm* means medicine. Gilead was a town referred to in Jeremiah 8:22. This town was famous for the spices and ointment which were developed from plants growing by the Jordan River. But Israel was so corrupted by its sin that the balm of Gilead was not efficacious. The universal balm is Jesus Christ and that balm is efficacious for all who believe in him.

Everyone who calls upon the name of the Lord will be saved (Acts 2:21) but not necessarily healed.

---

[93]Clarke, *Commentary*, 5:104.

[94]Erickson, *Christian Theology*, 839-841.

Perfect health is not a present, but a future benefit of the atonement. Physical healing is a foretaste of the resurrection of the body. If God has the power to raise from the dead, he has power to heal the sick.

However, Wesley did not advocate an attitude of resignation — that sickness was sent by God and should be borne in submission. Nor does Methodist theology embrace a cessationist view that miracles were only for the first century.

Wesley viewed medicine as a providential gift. In his day the term *physic* meant medical advice and his use of *primitive* was in reference to the practices of the early church. His book, *Primitive Physic*, opens by rehearsing human rebellion in Eden and the suffering and death which followed. But Wesley asserted that God neither abandoned us to infirmity nor rendered us completely passive in its treatment.[95]

Over time, Wesley grew more convinced that God's ultimate healing work extended to both soul and body. He encouraged his followers to expect both dimensions of healing in the present life. In a letter he wrote,

> Give yourself up to the Great Physician, that He may heal soul and body together. And unquestionably this is His design. He wants to give you and my dear Mrs. Knox both inward and outward health. . . . Look up, and wait for happy days![96]

---

[95] Wesley, *BE Works*, 32:21, 30-31, 111.

[96] Wesley, *Letter* to Alexander Knox, 26 Oct 1778.

Wesley believed that healing could come through medicine and through prayer. He believed that God has more than one method of healing either the soul or the body.[97] Accounts of miraculous healings are sprinkled throughout his *Journal.*

But Wesley put more emphasis on the ordinary means of maintaining and restoring health than he did on supernatural healing. Here again we see the moderation between the two polar opposites. While Calvinism tends to assert that the age of miracles is over, and the charismatic movement purports to cast out the demon of gluttony, Wesley advised his people to take responsibility for their health and trust God for healing. He advocated hygiene, diet, exercise, emotional health, and prayer. "I earnestly advise everyone, together with all his other medicines, to use that medicine of medicines, *prayer.*" He called prayer the universal medicine.[98]

Thus, if a Christian is ill, he should take an aspirin and pray. If he does not get relief, he should see his doctor and pray. We should not demand that God do supernaturally what can be done through the natural means which he has instituted. All healing comes from God, whether naturally or supernaturally.

However, when the ministry of the medical community has reached an impasse, the Christian should call for prayer at his local assembly. The procedure outlined in James 5:14-16 does not assume that anointing the sick is the specialized ministry of a

---

[97]Wesley, *Journal*, 18 May 1772.

[98]Wesley, *BE Works*, 32:404-405.

professional faith healer. Rather, it is assumed to be part of the worship in a local body of believers.

For the child of God, the future breaks into the present in the kingdom of God. And while divine healing is possible now, then there will be a general resurrection. We are *already* in the kingdom and have tasted the power of the world to come (Heb 6:5), but we are still under the curse of sin, and our bodies will die regardless of what we confess. However, Isaiah 65:20 implies that health will improve as the kingdom advances.

The influence of the gospel will bring healing to the nations of the world. Thus, the healing through Christ extends beyond mere physical healing which would be temporary and personal. Second Chronicles 7:14 promises the healing of the land of God's covenant people. God will flood this world with his Spirit and bring healing to the nations (Ezek 47:1-12; Rev 22:2).

Kimberly Alexander observed that healing, in the Wesleyan-Holiness tradition, is viewed as a sign of the coming kingdom, while the Finished Work Pentecostal tradition believed that healing was already accomplished on the cross, waiting to be appropriated by faith. Thus, there is tension between the *already* and the *not yet*.[99]

Knight concluded that we need a theology of healing that maintains the tension between God's faithfulness and freedom, between the *already* and the *not yet*. For Wesley,

---

[99]Alexander, *Pentecostal Healing,* 203-234.

Healing was important, because it was important to a loving God who will ultimately put an end to sickness and death. But it was not as important as salvation itself. . . . Consequently to elevate healing to the level of salvation is as great an error as to ignore it.[100]

Van Baalen referred to the "unpaid bills of the church." He argued that elements of truth which become neglected by the church tend to become distorted by cults. He concluded that the rise of many mind-healing and faith-healing cults is the result of the church not preaching a balanced message that God is the healer of the body as well as the soul.[101]

---

[100]Knight, *Anticipating Heaven Below*, 181-182.

[101]Van Baalen, *The Chaos of Cults*, 390, 393.

Future Benefits of the Atonement

According to Romans 8:18-25, all creation, except those members of the human race who are finally impenitent, will be influenced by the glory reflected from the children of God. While it was Adam who subjected the creation to this bondage, it will be through the redeemed of Adam's race that the creation will be released.

Wesley preached that creation and all the elements were off course and fighting against man. Man's sin cut the rest of creation off from the blessings of God. Just as man lost his perfection, so the beasts lost their perfection, which included a "loving obedience to man." The beasts became savage and cruel, destroying the weaker and being destroyed by man. But nothing can be clearer than the fact that they will not always remain in this condition.[102]

Mickelsen wrote that "tornadoes, hurricanes, earthquakes, drought, floods are just a few evidences of the imbalance of nature." While part of the world suffers drought, another part is flooded. But God has promised that "the very creation which has been enslaved to deterioration and corruption will be set

---

[102]This paragraph is a summary of Wesley, "The General Deliverance," Sermon #60.

free from this condition."[103]

Thus, Paul personifies creation in order to illustrate the cosmic significance of man's fall and the believer's restoration. Romans 8:19 contains a compound word ἀπεκδέχομαι (*apekdechomai*), made up of ἀπό (*apo* - from) + κάρα (*kara* - the head) + δοκέω (*dokeo* - to watch). Translated *earnest expectation* in the KJV, this word depicts watching with outstretched head; to strain forward for an eagerly awaited event. The prefix *apo* adds the idea of watching with concentration for that which is anticipated, emphasizing the difference between the present and future. The word, in its noun form, is found only here and in Philippians 1:20. J. B. Phillips translated it, "the whole creation is on tiptoe."[104] The creation waits in eager expectation and preparedness—all of which is implied in the verb again in Romans 8:23, 25.

Binney wrote that *vanity* means frustration, emptiness, aimlessness, suffering and death.[105] It is the same word for *vanity* in the Septuagint, the Greek translation of Ecclesiastes. It is used by Paul only in Romans 8:20, 1:21. The creation, at this present time, is unable to achieve the purpose for which it was created (see Gen 3:17-19). Yet in spite of its limitations and apparent purposelessness, nature still declares the attributes of God (Rom 1:20). Beet concluded that Romans 8:19-22 suggest "the earth beneath our feet, rescued from the curse of sin, will be

---

[103]Mickelsen, *Wycliffe Bible Commentary*, 1207.

[104]Phillips, *New Testament in Modern English*, 324.

[105]Binney, *TPC*, 413.

our eternal home."[106]

The entire creation was subjected to this suffering through Adam's choice. The verb *was subjected* is in the passive voice, indicating that creation was acted upon. However, the text does not indicate who did the acting. According to Genesis 3:17, God cursed the ground, which indicates that it was God who brought the creation under this frustration. But the One who brought the frustration also promised hope. The hope of final salvation also includes the liberation of the entire creation.

Christians have the firstfruits of the Spirit. But they also groan along with the rest of creation, suffering under the curse of sin. While we have already been adopted, we are not yet recipients of our full inheritance. We who are now adopted internally await the final, external phase, the redemption of our bodies. While we are *now* the sons of God, the world does not yet recognize us (1 John 3:1-2). Someday the true identity of the sons of God will be revealed (Rom 8:19) and their inheritance fully realized.

Revealed is ἀποκάλυψις (*apocalupsis*), the same word which begins the book of Revelation. The true identity of the sons of God will be revealed when we regain the dominion over the earth which Adam lost. "The liberation of all creation awaits the apocalypse of man, man's assumption of his dominion mandate," wrote Rushdoony.[107] Along with creation, we are also on tiptoes, in eager anticipation (Rom 8:19, 23) of our revelation, which is our public adoption by God.

---

[106]Beet, *Commentary*, 237.

[107]Rushdoony, *Romans & Galatians*, 137.

Romans 8:23 ties this to the redemption of our bodies, which refers to the general resurrection following Christ's return. While deliverance, in an absolute sense, will not occur until the second advent, there can be a progressive deliverance, leading up to that climatic event, as the world realizes the victory of the cross.

Creation was implicated by Adam's fall. The new redeemed race will be used by God to release all creation. Science and technology are not the savior of the world. The salvation offered which Christ alone brings, however, it is not limited to the spiritual nature of man. Victory over sin, in the regenerate, is just the start. Through his Spirit he enables his people to bring his grace and truth into every sphere of creation. Someday the meek will inherit the earth. Believers will realize their full authority. The emphasis in this passage, Romans 8:18-25, is not upon the destruction, but upon the transformation of the world.

The gospel not only provides a present deliverance from sin but a future hope of glory (Col 1:27). Christianity alone offers hope for all of God's creation. We alone understand creation's groan as the pain of childbirth. A new world is coming (2 Pet 3:13).

BIBLIOGRAPHY

Abraham, William. "Atonement." *Global Wesleyan Dictionary of Theology*. Al Truesdale, ed. Beacon Hill, 2013.

Alexander, Kimberly Ervin. *Pentecostal Healing: Models in Theology and Practice*. Deo, 2006.

Anselm. *Cur Deus Homo?* AD 1094-1098.

Archer, Gleason L. *A Survey of Old Testament Introduction*. Moody, 1974.

Arminius, James. *The Works of James Arminius*. 3 vols. The London Edition. 1825-1875. Reprint, Baker, 1996.

Athanasius. *Selected Works and Letters: A Select Library of Nicene and Post-Nicene Fathers of the Christian Church*. Second Series. Vol. 4. Philip Schaff and Henry Wace, eds. 1891. Reprint, Eerdmans, 1978. [*NPNF*]

Beet, Joseph Agar. *A Commentary on St. Paul's Epistle to the Romans*. 10th ed. 1902. Reprint, Allegheny, 1982.

Berkhof, Louis. *Systematic Theology*. Eerdmans, 1941.

Binney, Amos and Daniel Steele. *The People's Commentary on the New Testament*. Eaton & Mains, 1878.

Bounds, Christopher T. "The Scope of the Atonement in the Early Church Fathers." *Wesleyan Theological Journal* 47:2 (Fall 2012) 7-26.

Bright, John. *The Kingdom of God*. Abingdon, 1953.
Calvin, John. *Calvin's Commentaries*. 22 vos. 1540-1565. Reprint, Baker, 1979.
Carson, D. A. *Divine Sovereignty and Human Responsibility*. Baker, 1994.
Clarke, Adam. *The Miscellaneous Works of Adam Clarke*. 13 vols. T. Tegg, 1836-1837.
_____. *The Holy Bible, Containing the Old and New Testaments: The Text Carefully Printed from the Most Correct Copies of the Present Authorized Translations, Including the Marginal reading and Parallel Tests; with a Commentary and Critical Notes, Designed as a help to a Better Understanding of the Sacred Writings*. 6 vols. 1811-1825. Reprint, Abingdon, 1950.
_____. *The Miscellaneous Works of Adam Clarke*. 13 vols. James Everett, ed. London: Thomas Tegg, 1836-1837.
Coke, Thomas. *A Commentary on the Holy Bible*. 6 vols. G. Whitfield, 1801-1803.
Coppedge, Allan. *John Wesley in Theological Debate*. Wesley Heritage, 1987.
Denney, James. *The Death of Christ*. 1902. Reprint, Tyndale, 1951.
_____. *The Atonement and the Modern Mind*. A. C. Armstrong & Son, 1903.
Dunlap, Eldon Dale. "Methodist Theology in Great Britain." PhD diss, Yale University, 1956.
Douty, Norman. *Did Christ Die Only for the Elect: A Treatise on the Extent of Christ's Atonement*. Wipf & Stock, 1998.
Elwell, Walter A. "Extent of Atonement." *Evangelical Dictionary of Theology*. 3rd ed. Daniel J. Trier and

Walter A. Elwell, eds. Baker, 2016.

Erickson, Millard J. *Christian Theology*. Baker, 1985.

Fee, Gordon D. *The Disease of the Health and Wealth Gospel*. Word for Today, 1979.

Field, Benjamin. *The Student's Handbook of Christian Theology*. 1886. Reprint, Fountain, 1957.

Fletcher, John. *The Works of the Reverend John Fletcher*. 1833. Reprint, Schmul, 1974.

Gregory, Benjamin. "The Annual Address of the Conference to the Methodist Societies." *The Wesleyan Methodist Magazine* 94 (1871) 833-837.

Grudem, Wayne. *Systematic Theology*. Zondervan, 1994.

Knight, Henry H. III. *Anticipating Heaven Below: Optimism of Grace from Wesley to the Pentecostals*. Cascade, 2014.

Lewis, C. S. *The Screwtape Letters*. Macmillan, 1943.

Lightner, Robert P. "For Whom Did Christ Die?" *Walvoord: A Tribute*. Donald K. Campbell, ed. Moody, 1982.

_____. *The Death Christ Died: A Case for Unlimited Atonement* Revised ed. Kregel, 1998.

McGonigle, Herbert Boyd. *Sufficient Saving Grace: John Wesley's Evangelical Arminianism*. Paternoster, 2001.

Michelsen, A. Berkeley. "Romans." *The Wycliffe Bible Commentary*. Evert F. Harrison, ed. Moody, 1962.

Moo, Douglas J. *New International Commentary on the New Testament: Romans*. Eerdmans, 1996.

Morris, Leon. *The Atonement: It's Meaning and Significance*. InterVarsity, 1983.

Motyer, J. Alex. *Tyndale Old Testament Commentaries: Isaiah*. InterVarsity, 1999.

Moulton, James H. and George Milligan. *Vocabulary of*

the Greek Testament. 1915. Reprint, Hendrickson, 1977.

Noble, Thomas, A. "The 'Necessity' of Anselm: The Argument of the *Cur Deus Homo*." *Wesleyan Theological Journal* 50:1 (Spring 2015) 53-66.

_____. *Christian Theology*. Vol 1. *The Grace of our Lord Jesus Christ*. The Foundry, 2022.

North, Gary. "Common Grace, Eschatology, and Biblical Law." *The Journal of Christian Reconstruction* 3:2 (Winter 1976-1977) 13-47.

Oden, Thomas C. *The Word of Life: Systematic Theology: Volume Two*. Harper & Row, 1989.

_____. *Life in the Spirit: Systematic Theology: Volume Three*. HarperCollins, 1992.

_____. *The Transforming Power of Grace*. Abingdon, 1993.

Osborne, Grant R. "General Atonement View." *Perspectives on the Extent of the Atonement: Three Views*. Andrew David Naselli and Mark A. Snoeberger, eds. B&H, 2015.

Phillips, J. B. *Letters to Young Churches*. Macmillian, 1947.

Pope, William Burt. *A Compendium of Christian Theology*. 3 vols. Wesleyan Conference Office, 1880.

_____. *The Person of Christ*. Wesleyan Conference Office, 1871.

Ralston, Thomas N. *Elements of Divinity*. 1924. Reprint, Schmul, 1971.

Reasoner, Vic. "Golden Chain or Iron Padlock?" *The Arminian Magazine* 20:1 (Spring 2002) 1-2.

Rushdoony, Rousas John. *Romans & Galatians*. Ross House, 1997.

Sanders, Fred. "Wesleyan View." *Five Views on the Ex-*

tent of the Atonement. Zondervan, 2019.

Schreiner, Thomas R. *1-2 Peter, Jude*. Broadman & Holman, 2003.

_____. and Bruce A. Ware, eds. *Still Sovereign: Contemporary Perspectives on Election, Foreknowledge, and Grace*. Baker, 2004.

Scott, Leland Howard. "Methodist Theology in American in the Nineteenth Century." PhD diss, Yale University, 1954.

Shedd, William G. T. *Dogmatic Theology*. 3 vols. 1888. Reprint, Zondervan, 1988-1994.

Steele, Daniel. *A Substitute for Holiness or Antinomianism Revived; or the Theology of the So-Called Plymouth Brethren Examined and Refuted*. 3rd ed. Reprint, Schmul, 1980.

Stott, John R. W. *The Cross of Christ*. InterVarsity, 1986.

Summers, Thomas O. *Systematic Theology*. 2 vols. John Tigert, ed. Methodist Episcopal Church, South, 1888.

Taylor, Richard S. *God's Integrity and the Cross*. Francis Asbury, 1999.

Tooley, W Andrew. "Reinventing Redemption: The Methodist Doctrine of Atonement in Britain and America in the Long Nineteenth Century." PhD diss. University of Sterling, 2013.

Treffry, Richard, Jr. *Letters on the Atonement*. 2nd ed. 1845. Reprint, Schmul, 2021.

Trueman, Carl R. "Definite Atonement View." *Perspectives on the Extent of the Atonement: Three Views*. Andrew David Naselli and Mark A. Snoeberger, eds. B&H, 2015.

Van Baalen, Jan Karel. *The Chaos of Cults*. 4th ed.

Eerdmans, 1964.
Watson, Richard. *Theological Institutes.* 2 vols. 1823-1829. Reprint, Hunt & Eaton, 1889.

_____. *An Exposition of the Gospels of St. Matthew and St. Mark.* Wesleyan Conference Office. 1833.

Wesley, John. *The Bicentennial Edition of the Works of John Wesley.* 35 vols when complete. Nashville: Abingdon, 1976-.

_____, *Explanatory Notes Upon the New Testament.* 1754. Reprint, Schmul, 1976.

Whedon, Daniel D. *Commentary on the New Testament.* 5 vols. 1860-1880. Reprint, Schmul, 1977-1978.

Wiley, H. Orton. *Christian Theology.* 3 vols. Beacon Hill, 1940-1943.

Williams, Collin. *John Wesley's Theology Today.* Abingdon, 1960.

Witherington, Ben III. *Paul's Letter to the Romans: A Socio-Rhetorical Commentary.* Eerdmans, 2004.

_____. "The Death of Sin in the Death of Jesus: Atonement Theology in the N. T." *Wesleyan Theological Journal* 50:1 (Spring 2015) 7-22.

www.ingramcontent.com/pod-product-compliance
Lightning Source LLC
Chambersburg PA
CBHW060351050426
42449CB00011B/2930